The Countries

Poland

Kate A. Furlong

ABDO Publishing Company

visit us at
www.abdopub.com

Published by ABDO Publishing Company, 4940 Viking Drive, Edina, Minnesota 55435.
Copyright © 2001 by Abdo Consulting Group, Inc. International copyrights reserved in
all countries. No part of this book may be reproduced in any form without written
permission from the publisher.

Printed in the United States.

Photo Credits: Corbis

Contributing Editors: Bob Italia and Tamara L. Britton
Art Direction & Maps: Neil Klinepier

Library of Congress Cataloging-in-Publication Data

Furlong, Kate A., 1977-
    Poland / Kate A. Furlong.
       p. cm. -- (Countries)
    Includes index.
    ISBN 1-57765-498-6
       1. Poland--Juvenile Literature. [1. Poland.] I. Title. II. Series.

DK4147 .F87 2001
943.8--dc21

                                                        00-048616

Contents

Czesc!

Hello from Poland! Poland is an ancient country in eastern Europe. It has lakes, mountains, plains, and many interesting plants and animals.

Throughout its history, Poland has been home to many different people. They have given Poland its rich foods, beautiful folk clothing, and special celebrations.

Farming is the largest part of Poland's **economy**. Poles also manufacture goods. And they mine minerals from the earth.

Polish cities are full of history. Poles get around in their cities by riding in trains and cars. Ships and airplanes provide other ways to travel.

Poland's government is a **democracy**. Its president and **prime minister** govern the country. The National Assembly creates Poland's laws. The Supreme Court assures that Poles receive fair treatment under the law.

Throughout its history, Poland has faced many difficulties. It has been the site of many conflicts and wars. This has made life hard for the Poles. But they have endured to build a strong Polish nation.

Czesc *from Poland!*

Fast Facts

OFFICIAL NAME: Republic of Poland (Rzeczpospolita Polska)

CAPITAL: Warsaw

LAND
- Mountain Ranges: Sudeten and Carpathian Mountains
- Highest Peak: Mount Rysy 8,199 feet (2,499 m)
- Major Rivers: Vistula and Odra Rivers

PEOPLE
- Population: 38,608,929 (2000 est.)
- Major Cities: Warsaw, Lodz, Krakow
- Official Language: Polish
- Religion: Roman Catholicism (unofficial)

GOVERNMENT
- Form: Parliamentary Republic
- Chief of State: President
- Head of Government: Prime minister
- Legislature: National Assembly (made up of the Sejm and the Senate)
- Flag: Two equal red and white bands running across the flag from left to right
- Symbol: Eagle
- Nationhood: November 11, 1918

ECONOMY
- Agricultural Products: Potatoes, fruits, vegetables, wheat; poultry, eggs, pork, beef, milk, cheese
- Mining Products: Coal, sulfur, barite, salt, kaolin, limestone, chalk, gypsum, marble, copper, zinc, iron, nickel, vanadium, cobalt, silver
- Manufactured Products: Machines, iron, steel, chemicals, ships, food, glass, beverages, textiles
- Money: Zloty (one hundred grosz equal one zloty)

Poland's flag

Poland's money is called the zloty. Zlotys are divided into 100 smaller units called grosz.

Timeline

966	Duke Mieszko I officially founds Poland
1333	Casimir III becomes king and restores order to Poland
1386	Jadwiga marries Jagiello; their marriage creates a mighty empire
1611	King Sigismund II makes Warsaw Poland's capital
1914	World War I begins
1918	World War I ends; Poland declares itself an independent nation
1939	World War II begins
1945	World War II ends; the Soviet Union controls Poland and makes it communist
1980	Poles organize a workers' union called Solidarity
1981–1983	Poland is under martial law
1989	Poland breaks free of communism and becomes a democracy
1997	Poland adopts a new constitution

Poland's Past

Piast Dynasty leader Duke Mieszko I (mee-EHZ-kah) officially founded Poland in A.D. 966. Under Mieszko's control, Poland grew to more than 1 million citizens. And Mieszko brought Christianity to Poland.

Mieszko died in 992. Piast leaders continued to rule Poland. Poland was weak and disorganized for years. Then in 1333, Casimir III became king. He **reunified** Poland. He encouraged Jews to move there. And he **annexed** parts of Russia. Casimir III died in 1370.

Princess Jadwiga (yuh-VEE-gah) was Poland's next important ruler. In 1386, she married Jagiello (yuh-GEEL-ah), a Lithuanian prince. Jagiello's family ruled Poland for 200 years. Then, Polish nobles decided to elect the king.

The elected kings faced problems. There were many wars. Poland's neighbors wanted its land. By 1795,

Austria, Prussia, and Russia had split all of Poland's land among them.

For the next 123 years, Poland did not exist. But it still lived in the spirit of the Polish people. During this time, they attempted to free Poland from its neighbors. But they were not successful.

Jozef Pilsudski

In 1914, **World War I** began in Europe. When the war ended, Poland's neighbors were weak. The Poles seized the chance to free their country. On November 11, 1918, Polish leader Jozef Pilsudski (yo-ZEHF peel-SOOT-skee) declared Poland an independent nation.

The Poles worked hard to rebuild their country. During this time, Poland's neighbor Russia had a revolution. Russia's name changed to the Soviet Union.

On August 23, 1939, the Soviet Union and Germany signed a secret agreement. It described how they would attack Poland. They wanted to divide Poland's land and people between Germany and the Soviet Union.

On September 1, 1939, Germany attacked Poland. This attack started **World War II**. Life grew hard for the Poles. The Germans killed many Polish leaders. Other Poles had to go to Germany and work in labor camps. Poland's Jewish people had to live in **ghettos**. And thousands were killed in **concentration camps**.

When the war ended, the Soviet Union controlled Poland. Poland had a **communist** government. Many Poles disliked the new government. So, the Poles started to strike.

Opposite page: A workers' strike at the Gdansk Shipyards in August of 1980 led to the creation of the Solidarity union.

In 1980, the Poles won the right to organize a workers' union. They called it Solidarity. Ten million workers joined Solidarity. It was a step toward **democracy**.

The **communist** government did not like Solidarity. So, in December 1981, Poland was put under martial law. The Poles had a curfew. Their mail and phone calls were censored. People who disagreed with the government were jailed.

Martial law lasted until July 1983. Then things slowly got better for the Poles. In 1989, Poland became the first Eastern European country to break free of communism.

In 1990, Poland had its first free election. The Poles elected Lech Walesa (LEHCK vah-WENZ-uh) as their president. They had worked hard and created a successful **democracy**.

Today, a new **constitution** governs Poland. It was written in 1997. It was Poland's first constitution since communist rule. Poles hope their new constitution and democratic government will create a strong Polish nation.

Lech Walesa

Poland's Great Land

Poland is in Europe. Northern Poland has rolling hills and valleys. They are covered by thick forests. This area also has most of Poland's lakes. Vast plains stretch across central Poland. The plains have rich soil and a long growing season.

The Sudeten and Carpathian (cahr-PAY-thee-uhn) Mountains rise along Poland's southern border. The Carpathians are made up of the Beskids and Tatras ranges. The Tatras have Poland's highest peak, Mount Rysy (RUH-suh).

The Tatras Mountains

North America
Europe
DETAIL AREA
Asia
Africa
South America
Australia
Antarctica

Estonia
Sweden
Latvia
Baltic Sea
Lithuania
Russia
POLAND
Belarus
Germany
Czech Republic
Ukraine
Slovakia
Austria
Hungary
Romania

BALTIC SEA
GDYNIA
GDANSK
SZCZECIN
Warta
Bug
River
Odra
River
Vistula
★ **WARSAW**
River
LODZ
River
KRAKOW
SUDETEN MOUNTAINS
CARPATHIAN MOUNTAINS
TATRAS MOUNTAINS
MOUNT RYSY

North
West ✦ East
South

Poland has many important waterways. All of Poland's rivers run north. They drain into the Baltic Sea. The country's longest river is the Vistula. It is 650 miles (1,047 km) long and runs through the middle of the country. Over 9,000 lakes also dot Poland's land.

Poland has four seasons. Spring starts in March. It has cool, windy, rainy weather. Summer starts in June. It is hot and sunny. Sometimes it rains. By September, fall weather is cool, windy, and foggy. Winter begins in December. It is cold and snowy.

The Vistula River

Rainfall

North

West — East

South

AVERAGE YEARLY RAINFALL

Inches		*Centimeters*
10 - 20		*25 - 50*
20 - 40		*50 - 100*
40 - 60		*100 - 150*

Temperature

Winter

Summer

AVERAGE TEMPERATURE

Fahrenheit		*Celsius*
50° - 68°		*10° - 20°*
32° - 50°		*0° - 10°*
Under 32°		*Under 0°*

The Natural World

Forests cover about a third of Poland. Most of the forests have pine trees. Oak, beech, birch, larch, and fir trees also grow in Poland's forests. The forests shelter many animals.

Bialowieza (bee-uh-lah-VEE-zuh) National Park is in eastern Poland. It is home to herds of European bison. Many bison once roamed across Poland. Today, they only live in protected areas.

Horses are another important animal in Poland. Poles are famous for breeding Arabian horses. These horses have won contests throughout the world.

Many birds live in Poland. The most common are sparrows, crows, magpies, skylarks, nightingales, and swallows. Northern Poland's lakes are home to mallard ducks, herons, and swans.

Each summer, thousands of white storks live in Poland. Most Poles like the storks. They believe storks bring good luck.

European bison

The Poles

Most people in Poland are Polish. Small communities of Ukrainians, Germans, Belorussians, and Jews also live there. Nearly every Pole speaks Polish. It is the official language.

Nearly all Poles are Roman Catholic. The Catholic Church has been powerful during Poland's history. In 1978, a Pole named Karol Wojyla (kuh-RAHL vah-JEH-luh) was elected pope. Wojyla is now known as Pope John Paul II.

Poland has a variety of rich, delicious foods. *Bigos* is made of **sauerkraut**, fresh cabbage, and several meats. *Pierogi* are dumplings stuffed with cheese, meat, cabbage, or mushrooms.

Poland has special traditional clothing. The women wear full skirts with brightly-colored stripes. Their blouses are embroidered with flowers. Men wear plain or striped pants. They wear white shirts with sleeveless coats.

Opposite page: Traditional Polish clothing is often worn on special occasions.

Polish children ages 7 through 18 must attend school. Poland has nursery schools, primary schools, and secondary schools. When students complete secondary school, they may attend a university. One of Poland's leading universities is the Jagiellonian (yuh-geel-oh-NEE-uhn) University. It has been teaching students since 1364.

In the country, Polish homes have much land and open space for crops. In the cities, most Poles live in tall apartment houses.

Barszcz

Barszcz is a delicious beet soup.

12 medium beets
1 qt. water
1 tbsp. sugar
salt and pepper

1 sliced onion
juice of 1 lemon
2 cups vegetable bouillon
1/2 cup sour cream

Wash and peel the beets. Cook the beets and onion in water until the beets are tender. Add lemon juice, sugar, salt, and pepper. Refrigerate overnight. Strain and add bouillon. Heat, add sour cream, and serve.

AN IMPORTANT NOTE TO THE CHEF: Always have an adult help with the preparation and cooking of food. Never use kitchen utensils or appliances without adult permission and supervision.

English	Polish
Yes	Tak
No	Nie
Thank You	Dziekuje
Please	Prosze
Hello	Czesc
Goodbye	Do Widzenia
You're Welcome	Prosze

LANGUAGE

Earning a Living

After **World War II**, Poland's **communist** government controlled the **economy**. This meant the government owned many of Poland's businesses.

When Poland broke free of communism in 1989, the economy changed. The government had less control over the economy. So, more Polish people were able to own businesses.

Farming is a valuable part of the Polish economy. Polish farmers harvest potatoes, sugar beets, rye, wheat, and barley. Farmers also raise pigs.

Poland's land has many minerals. Coal is Poland's leading mineral. It is mined in eastern Poland. Sulfur is another important mineral. Poland has some of the world's largest sulfur mines. Copper and zinc are other important minerals.

Many Poles manufacture goods. They make steel, chemicals, glass, fabric, paper, appliances, and cars. People in coastal cities build ships. Many of these ships are exported to other countries.

About half of Poland's land is fit to grow crops.

Warsaw, Lodz, & Krakow

Warsaw is Poland's capital city. It is located on the Vistula River. In 1611, King Sigismund III made Warsaw Poland's capital.

Warsaw is a busy, modern city. It is home to 1.6 million people. They can relax by visiting their city's beautiful parks and museums.

The city of Lodz (WOO-zuh) is southwest of Warsaw. Lodz is Poland's second-largest city. It is an important textile producer. Poland's film industry is also centered in Lodz. It is called the Polish Hollywood. The city also has flourishing art and music communities.

Krakow (KRUH-kahv) is Poland's third-largest city. It is rich in history. Its marketplace, called Rynek Glowny (reh-NEHK GLAHV-neh), has been serving customers since the 1200s. St. Mary's Church has a beautiful altar and stained glass windows from the 1300s.

For more than 500 years, Polish kings ruled from Krakow's famous Wawel (vuh-VEL) Castle.

From Here to There

There are 14,900 miles (24,000 km) of railways in Poland. They crisscross the country, connecting Poland's major cities. The trains transport people and goods. They also connect Poland with its neighbors.

Poland's roadways carry cars and buses. Poles drive their cars on modern highways to get from place to place. Local buses make stops in neighborhoods. Other buses carry riders across the country.

Waterways transport many Polish goods. The shipping industry is strong in Poland. Its three largest ports are Szczecin (shch-eh-SEEN), Gdynia (guh-deen-EH-uh), and Gdansk (guh-DUHNSK). Ferries connect Poland to Sweden and Denmark.

The government runs Poland's airline. It is called Polskie Linie Lotnicze (pol-SKEE lee-NEE-uh laht-NEEcheh), or LOT. LOT makes regular flights to and from Poland's major cities. It also flies to cities in other countries.

A passenger train in Poland

The Republic of Poland

From 1947 to 1989, Poland had a **communist** government. The Polish United Workers' Party (PUWP) controlled the government. It was Poland's only political party.

In 1989, Poland became a **parliamentary republic**. The PUWP no longer existed. New, **democratic** parties formed. Today, they govern the country.

Poland's government meets in Warsaw. The people elect the president. He or she serves as head of state for five years. The president names the **prime minister**.

Poland's lawmaking body is called the National Assembly. It is broken into two groups, the Sejm (SEH-jum) and the Senate. The Sejm has 460 members. The Senate has 100 members.

The highest Polish court is called the Supreme Court. Poland's **provinces** and districts have their own courts.

The National Assembly meets at this building in Warsaw.

Polish Celebrations

Christmas is an important holiday in Poland. People begin preparing for it weeks in advance. Poles usually celebrate Christmas Eve at home with family. They start to eat supper when the first star appears in the night sky. They share holy bread called *oplatek* (oh-PWA-tehk). Then, they eat a 12-course meal of traditional Polish food.

After supper, children open gifts under the Christmas tree. At midnight, families go to church to celebrate **mass**. On Christmas Day, Poles spend more time with family. They socialize and attend mass.

Easter is another important holiday in Poland. On Easter morning, Poles go to church to celebrate mass. Then they return home to have a delicious breakfast of bread, sausage, cake, and eggs. Usually the foods served for Easter breakfast have been blessed by a priest.

In the fall, farmers celebrate harvest festivals. Farmers and their families give thanks for their harvest and pray for continued good crops.

Girls carry wreaths made of corn. They do a special dance and give the wreaths to the farmers. The farmers will start the next year's planting with a few seeds from the wreath.

A harvest festival display and wreath

Polish Culture

Poland has a long history of beautiful music. One of the country's most famous composers is Frederic Chopin. He wrote music for the piano during the early 1800s. He wrote many polonaises (pahl-uh-NAZEZ) and mazurkas (mah-ZOOR-kuhz), which are kinds of Polish music.

The polonaise is slow, gliding music. Polish kings and queens danced to the polonaise during the 1600s, 1700s, and 1800s.

The mazurka is Polish folk music that began in the 1500s. Poles dance to the mazurka by forming a circle, stomping their feet, and clicking their heels.

Polonaises and mazurkas are still played in Poland today. Jazz, pop, opera, and classical music can be heard in Poland, too.

Not only is Poland known for its music, it is also known for its scientists. In the 1500s, Poland's Nicolaus Copernicus studied how the earth rotates in relation to the sun. In the early 1900s, Polish scientist Marie Curie won two **Nobel Prizes** for chemistry.

Marie Curie

Poland has produced many excellent writers, too. Two Polish writers have even won the Nobel Prize for literature. Czeslaw Milosz (CHEH-sluhv MEE-luhsh) won it in 1980. He is best known for his essays against **communism** called *The Captive Mind* (1953). Wislawa Szymborksa (VEES-luh-vuh SHEHM-buhrk-suh) won the **Nobel Prize** for literature in 1996. Her most famous work is a book of poetry called *View with a Grain of Sand* (1995).

Poland has preserved its folk culture in special, open-air museums called skansens. Skansen museums are set up to look like traditional Polish villages. Skansens have houses, barns, churches, mills, and other buildings. They are filled with traditional tools, decorations, and furniture. These items show visitors what Polish life was like many years ago.

Sports are a popular pastime in Poland. Many Poles enjoy spending time outside. In the mountains, there are hiking trails and campgrounds. The town of Zakopane in the Tatras Mountains is Poland's downhill skiing capital. In the summer, people enjoy boating and swimming in the country's many lakes. Soccer is another popular sport that draws large crowds.

Opposite page: A family enjoys hiking in the Bialowieza National Forest.

Glossary

annex - to add land to a country.

communism - an economic system in which everything is owned by the government and given to the people as they need it.

concentration camp - a camp where political enemies and prisoners of war are held. During World War II, many Jews were sent to concentration camps in Germany and Poland.

constitution - the laws that govern a country.

democracy - a form of government where the people hold the power. They elect officials to represent them.

economy - the way a country uses its money, goods, and natural resources.

ghetto - the part of a city where Jews were required to live during World War II.

mass - a worship celebration in the Catholic Church.

Nobel Prize - an award for someone who has made outstanding achievements in his or her field.

parliamentary republic - a type of government in which the power rests with voting citizens and is carried out by elected officials, such as a parliament.

prime minister - the chief minister in some governments.

province - a political division that is like a state.

reunify - to bring something back together again.

sauerkraut - finely chopped cabbage that is salted and allowed to sour.

World War I - 1914-1918. Fought in Europe. The United States, Great Britain, France, Russia, and their allies were on one side. Germany, Austria-Hungary, and their allies were on the other side. The war began when Archduke Ferdinand was assassinated.

World War II - 1939-1945. Fought in Europe, Asia, and Africa. The United States, Great Britain, France, the Soviet Union, and their allies were on one side. Germany, Italy, Japan, and their allies were on the other side. The war began when Germany invaded Poland.

Web Sites

Polish National Tourist Office
http://www.polandtour.org
Read more about Poland's history, geography, culture, and arts. Learn about Poland's mountains, parks, and provinces, and get information about traveling in Poland.

Embassy of Poland
http://www.polandembassy.org
Get the latest news on developments in Poland at this site from the Polish Embassy in Washington, D.C. Click on Virtual Tour to learn more about Polish history, famous Poles, sports, culture, and more!

These sites are subject to change. Go to your favorite search engine and type in "Poland" for more sites.

Index